Winning the Battle in My Mind and How:

A Journal for Emotional Health

To Help Gain VICTORY
Over What Gets You Down
(spiritual self healing book for trauma)

Inner Reformation

This Journal is For:

This book is dedicated to the
Three Holy Hearts and the author's children.

Contents

Introduction

5 years ago, I set out to thrive and DID NOT . . . . I've come to believe that the key to truly thriving is having peace as a baseline.

Hi, and welcome! My name is Tessa, and I'm a mother, friend, dancer, and theological thinker. I love to make art. I love to dance, pray, sing, and play. For much of my adult life, however, I've cried. In fact, I've spent years crying—sobbing over my life's situation. In every attempt to "get better," I only grew worse. At times, I've wanted to die, give up, and run away, but I'm still here, and I'm proud to report that I have finally begun to THRIVE. I finally feel HAPPY, even free.

Since my early twenties, I have wanted to write books and pamphlets to share my heart, ideas, and strategies for living, growing, and being. However, I never thought I would live to make it since my emotional suffering was so severe. But I am, and now my time has come to use my voice to SPEAK!—sharing all that is within me—praying and hoping that my life's journey will deeply touch and impact yours.

Why? Because I want you to thrive, too. I want you to live a whole, abundant life of joy, play, peace, freedom, and stability. I want you to GROW and live an incredible existence because I know how much it hurts to be emotionally, mentally, spiritually, and physically taxed.

In this book, I want us to journey together as we take steps towards greater, surer internal peace and calm. Here's to your health and wholeness as you work through this gentle journal step by step!

With Love,

From Your Friend,

Tessa

the creator of Inner Reformation

How To Use This Book

This 21-day journal encourages self-reflection, self-healing, and self-care. It's a health and wellness resource intended to foster internal peace and calm, enabling you to function better and live a happier, more fulfilling life with anxiety and fear kept at bay.

It's written to promote your internal rest and thriving (as well as external) so you can experience PEACE. In many ways, it is a mental health book or an emotional health journal, but you are steering the wheel to promote and gain your inward well-being and freedom (while not abandoning the external).

In this journal, I will share a little about my life and struggles—as well as some of my spiritual experiences and conversions—while guiding you through gentle, thoughtful questions about your life's journey. Throughout, I sincerely want to convey that you are good, capable, and lovable. My priest shares this message with his parishioners, and he once told us, "You are to tell this message."

Therefore, this book will be divided into three solid sections: one on self-reflection, self-healing, and self-care. Please work through it at a pace to calm and still your body and mind to feel more at ease, regulated, and confident in who you are and what you are about (I want you to feel good about yourself, your surroundings, and your life, especially if you are someone who has struggled for years like me). In this journal, we will work through negative thoughts, address false stories we tell ourselves, and discuss boundaries, fears, insecurities, and other related topics. We aim to do this within 21 days.

Overall, the goal is to feel greater rest and ease in body and mind throughout the day and life—during both the good and "bad"—and to provide tools for greater emotional resilience to empower you to direct your emotions and well-being thoughtfully. May this book bless you as you gently work through it, question by question. If you'd like more space to write, please use a notebook alongside this journal.

Also, yes, you see me in the images in this book. My art is meant to inspire you to create or appreciate the beauty that a simple image or pose can offer. Enjoy, and God bless!

Chapter One

Self-Reflection

Y ou are good.

The goal of this chapter is to increase self-confidence, especially for individuals who struggle with self-worth. Many of us struggle and feel terrible about ourselves and our lives for various reasons. Because of this, I want to encourage you in resting, feeling at ease, and developing Emotional Resilience in the face of trial (i.e., explore tools to recover from hardships, manage feelings, and have a more positive outlook).

It is recorded that Christ said, "Love your neighbor as yourself." My friend, you matter.

On the next page is a list of pain points and mental and emotional stresses that people aged 18-40+ experience. An emotional pain point is anything that disrupts our internal peace, safety, or relaxation (e.g., fears, insecurities, fatigue, relational issues, hunger, lack of sleep, anxiety, feeling overwhelmed, and so on).

Emotional Pain Points for Adults:

Negative Self-Talk—persisting negative thoughts and self-doubt that a person says, often unknowingly, in their mind.

Stress and Anxiety—chronic unrest that can be related to work, relationships, and life transitions.

Lack of Focus—difficulty concentrating or staying motivated due to mental clutter or overactivity.

Fear of Failure—an overwhelming concern that can keep people from taking risks or pursuing desired goals.

Feeling Overwhelmed—overstimulation by unexpected challenges or daily responsibilities.

Struggles with Self-Discipline—having trouble maintaining routines or habits that foster the well-being of our soul.

These are a few internal struggles that humans face, which can sometimes keep us feeling stuck, sad, disconnected, or discontented. For example, when such hardships become habitual or unmanageable, we can easily feel like we're trapped, as if life will never change or improve. Over the next seven days for Chapter One, I would like to do some gentle, thoughtful self-reflection to help us feel more in control of our thoughts, emotions, well-being, and, hopefully, our surroundings. Our questions will first focus inwardly and progress outwardly throughout the chapter.

Here we go!

Day 1

Question: At present, what things do you struggle with? What takes away your peace and joy? Are there certain things you long to change or wish to feel differently about? Note: This could include several topics, but that's okay. Please be thorough but gentle as you answer in the space provided.

Closing thought: No matter what you are going through, I know it can seem overwhelming at times or near impossible, but somehow life can improve, and you are exceptional. Please keep pressing forward, and may you feel more peace within your spirit. I'm rooting for you!

Day 2

Question: Today, we will explore how you feel about yourself and your well-being at this time. Specifically, on any given day, are you highly critical of who you are? For example, do you find that negative thoughts and negative self-talk consume you, or is your thought life fairly positive? I'm gently inviting us to notice: How aware are you of your emotions? Do you sometimes disconnect from them? Lastly, off the top of your head, how would you like to GROW emotionally and mentally? These are a lot of questions, so please take your time.

Closing thought: If you regularly have a hopeful, positive mental and emotional outlook, that is wonderful—congratulations! May those aspects continue to grow. If you find yourself repeating negative thoughts, speaking negatively about yourself, your life, or others, please know that it is possible to overcome. I'm living proof of that. Again, I'm rooting for you. Bless you!

Day 3

Question: Today, we're going to go a little deeper by asking: Do you often feel at rest and ease in your body and spirit? Does your physical body feel calm and relaxed, or do you frequently feel stressed and overwhelmed? I gently ask, do you habitually deal with anxiety or anxious thoughts, or, on the contrary, do you often feel assured and confident?

What's your internal landscape like—mentally, emotionally, or even spiritually? What is your body communicating? In other words, do you perceive you need more rest and ease? Maybe more adventure and play? Note: The questions in this chapter are currently serving as an emotional check-in to build greater self-awareness for the sake of well-being. There are many questions here, so please choose and select what's best for you.

Closing thought: The body speaks. Like listening to our thoughts and feelings, it's beneficial that we hear holistically. For example, when considering our limits and needs, we can learn. In other words, our bodies can surprisingly convey the information we need regarding sleep, food, connecting with others, being outdoors, being playful, and being joyful. As we reflect gently, it's important that we consider this "built-in" system of information instead of chronically allowing it to be dismissed. More on this to come :)

Day 4

Question: Stress, anxiety, depression, PTSD, CPTSD, body dysmorphia—all of these things and more can be caused by multiple factors. Perhaps a common link in many of them, however, is unresolved trauma. You might ask, "What is trauma?" since it's currently a frequently used term. Trauma can be anything that overwhelms your nervous system, causing you to struggle to understand what has occurred, lose connection with those you care about, or lose the ability to choose or control a particular outcome or circumstance in your life that you would like or don't want. I'll share how I learned about trauma and its definition at the end of this book. Sadly, trauma can leave us emotionally and mentally tender because it so easily overstimulates, frightens, or threatens our well-being; it can include any event—large or small—that overwhelms our bodies and/or greatly disappoints our yearnings and desires, such as losing something that we love or a mishap occurring that we didn't anticipate.

With this in mind, I know it's a lot to process, but are there particular events that have impacted you, affecting your feelings, spirit, and well-being? Again, such things can seem minor, but if they trouble you or never seem to go away, they're genuinely worth considering. I humbly ask, did those events occur during childhood, adolescence, adulthood, or perhaps in all of the above? How do these traumas impact you presently? Note: It can be common to dismiss things we deem "insignificant" or not as dire, but, again, if it has burdened you, it's worth consideration. Thus, please be gentle when answering, as we don't want to overwhelm our hearts and minds.

Closing thought: When struggling with anxiety, depression, PTSD, among other things, it's easy to feel ashamed or be upset that we somehow can't "get it together." My friend, as we reflect, being gentle with ourselves is essential because I can almost say with certainty that unresolved traumas in our lives impact the heart, mind, soul, and body on a daily, weekly, monthly, and yearly basis. Though you may feel like it, you're not silly to be affected by the things that hurt. In fact, as someone who taught me says, it makes perfect sense that you would feel that way. May we experience wholeness and safety in our lives. You matter, and you are good.

Storytime

In my adolescence, I experienced a significant rejection and trauma: I lost the person that I loved the most. That loss and rejection worked in tandem with the rocky relationship and divorce of my parents. For the next 20 years, I struggled incessantly over losing the person that I once loved. I never thought I would heal from that rejection and former relationship, but as God would have it, I did. It took loads of work and prayer, but it happened over time, and I'm stronger and wiser for it.

Day 5

Question: What was and is your family of origin like? Did you feel seen and heard growing up, or were you generally dismissed? Was the atmosphere in your home loving and supportive? Can you gently tell me a little about your family and upbringing? Note: We're examining this topic because, believe it or not, your upbringing powerfully impacts who you are today—your emotions, mental state, spirituality, and your ability to connect with others and yourself. At the end of this book, I'll provide resources to learn about "Attachment Theory" from someone who has greatly helped me in life to heal. This theory could be particularly helpful to you, as our upbringing significantly influences how we connect with others. Clue: People desperately desire "secure attachments" rather than forming unhealthy relationships. Again, we'll talk about this more later. For now, please answer the above questions in the space provided.

Day 6

Question: I've emphasized that our family of origin and former traumas can impact our physical, spiritual, mental, and emotional health, but even our education or society's structure can eventually order our lives in ways that sadly bring us harm. Over time, these experiences or "systems" can erode our self-perception, our view of the world, and our life circumstances. Here's a big question: What systems have let you down throughout the years, if any, and how can that be lovingly rectified? Some examples include education, healthcare, government, and religious institutions. I ask, how do you gracefully move forward when what you thought was true or correct—based on what the system told you to be true—is no longer the way? Again, please be gentle as you work through such thoughts. I'm rooting for you.

Closing thought: It's okay if we change or take a different route than we expected to keep growing and moving forward. Decision-making and following through take courage. I'm proud of you for discerning the peaceful path you need to take to move forward in life. Bless you and hug.

Day 7

Question: In this chapter, we've focused on self-reflection. We've done this by examining our lives and current challenges, pondering negative self-talk, our family upbringing, and traumas, as well as considering systems and how to move forward thoughtfully. The focus of this chapter is "**You are Good.**" I desire for you to grow in confidence, all while gaining greater internal rest and peace to navigate life. You matter, and you are significant. Christians believe that when the world was created, God pronounced it "GOOD." This includes you. Yet, this concept is often difficult to grasp, mainly because many messages we receive in life emphasize the opposite. While there's a lot of heartache and imperfection, the reality remains: you are a living being who possesses so much potential. Despite the negativity, challenging upbringings, past traumas, current hardships, and the like, how can we (i.e., you) nurture your God-given goodness within? How can you let go of outside forces that desperately try to bring you down, suggesting you are less than who and what you are? Note: This chapter began with inward self-reflection and moved outward to the consideration of family, systems, and trauma. Today's questions combine the inward with the outward for the sake of our growth. If you need more space to write, there's more on the back of the next page.

Tools

As we close Chapter One, what tools can I leave you with to promote your internal relaxation and rest to gain better emotional resilience for the sake of confidence? Thankfully, I've found some resources that have helped me immensely, so I will share:

1. Going outdoors, being connected to the earth, feeling the wind and sunshine, smelling flowers, and seeing fellow creatures or nature on a walk can calm our bodies. Fresh air can do wonders for the spirit when we feel down, troubled, sad, or blue. For example, it can help take us out of racing thoughts, allowing us to be present in our bodies—to feel more calm and relaxed. Being outdoors can be regulating.

2. Increased knowledge of the nervous system can help us better direct our emotions and actions. How? Thoroughly learning about the nervous system teaches us that what we are emotionally experiencing is, in fact, connected to our body. In other words, the nervous system directly impacts our mood, thoughts, and actions, and as shared, can be linked to unresolved trauma. At the end of this book, I will guide you to specific resources to learn about the nervous system and how to get in the "driver's seat" of your thoughts and feelings, as taught by Sarah Baldwin.

Chapter Two

Self-Healing

Y ou are capable.

The goal of this chapter is to promote your healing holistically, especially for those who suffer with aching hearts. When researching demographics for this book, the "Desired Benefits" of the reader kept coming up. For those of us who struggle with emotional health, what are we looking for? We long for wholeness, happiness, contentment, meaning, security, and more. I'll provide a list to break it down further.

Desired Mental and Emotional Benefits of the Reader:

Mental Clarity—we want clarity in thoughts, mind, and heart by reducing mental clutter to help with decision-making.

Better Emotional Resilience—we desire tools to help us recover from challenges and regulate our emotions, thoughts, and feelings.

More Self-Confidence—we would like to overcome self-doubt and be assured of our talents, gifts, who we are, and life purpose.

Enhanced Focus and Productivity—society teaches us to succeed in personal development and professional tasks, but we also require rest, regaining of strength, and play.

Practical Coping Skills—we desire techniques for managing our daily anxiety and stress.

Empowerment—we want our emotions and actions to be carefully guided so we aren't seemingly ruled by something other than ourselves, being in the "driver's seat" of how we respond.

These are a few areas of emotional growth that people long for. Thus, over the next seven days in Chapter Two, we'll again address our thought life and connect it to the body (to our nervous system). Like our previous reflection on negative self-talk, this time we'll discuss false stories we tend to tell ourselves and the need to "reframe" them. Additionally, we'll address fears and insecurities, aiming to bring healing and restoration into our lives by focusing on "You are capable."

Here we go!

Day 8

Question: Being unaware of our thoughts is easy. It takes practice to become "self-aware." Part of self-awareness is listening to what we need, what is lacking in our lives, or what is too much. In Chapter One, I asked you to consider your thoughts and whether you think critically of yourself or not. It took me many years to realize what I was feeling and examine why I was having numerous negative inclinations. In this process, I discovered that I was telling myself false stories about myself and certain events in my life. Some of the negative stories we unintentionally repeat can include: "I'll never make it," "No one will ever love me," "I'm too this or that," or "I'm not good enough." "I'm not pretty enough," "My life is never going to change," "I'm a failure," and so on. These repetitive thought narratives—often unknowingly present in our minds unless we're aware—can define us in many ways, setting us back or keeping us stuck in a critical feedback loop of ourselves, others, and our circumstances. Thankfully, life doesn't have to be this way: repetitive, negative thoughts can be minimized with practice. Again, we'll discuss that in this chapter. For now, please consider what, if any, negative stories you habitually rehearse regarding yourself, others, or your story. Please write that down, and be specific if you can, to build awareness.

Day 9

Question: Humans are meaning-making creatures. What I mean is we like to make meaning, and we do this to "make sense" of our lives. For example, when an event happens, we gradually form stories in our minds to arrange our thoughts, actions, and lives, but what happens when the meaning we make isn't the whole picture or the truth? Example: Someone rejects you or doesn't love you back to the degree that you love them. As a result, you form a false conclusion in your mind about yourself and what happened, leading to self-hatred or a complete blame shift to the other person, while neglecting to see your role in the matter. Humans continually make meaning and form opinions about the events in their lives. Sadly, sometimes the meanings we conclude can be misleading about what occurred or what is so, especially concerning ourselves and our character (or another person's character).

For those of us who are hard on ourselves or have perfectionist tendencies, negative stories and false conclusions can hamper our lives and well-being. For those inclined to blame others falsely, sadly, their sense of superiority can increase. What I want to emphasize on Day Nine is this: whatever negative stories or meanings unknowingly form in our minds, often those narratives can result from trauma. Yesterday, I asked you to consider repetitive, negative thoughts that you unintentionally repeat, such as "I'm so messed up. I'm too far gone. I'm never going to make it." Today, I ask if those repetitive thought patterns are at all related to the traumas you've already mentioned in this book, and if so, how? How can you "reframe" those repeated negative stories about yourself, others, or your situation? In other words, what could you say positively instead of them, or how could you look at matters more holistically?

Day 10

Question: Dear one, I desperately desire for negative or critical thoughts about yourself, others, or your life to gradually dissolve. We don't have to look at the world with rose-colored glasses, believing everything is positive. No. We can see things as they are: challenging, messy, and beautiful. Since I'm not an expert, I'll direct you to the experts at the end of this book. However, as mentioned, learning about the nervous system can help resolve the emotional tension we feel. How? The thoughts we think, our actions, and the narratives we tell ourselves result from our internal landscape (i.e., how our nervous system is or isn't functioning). As experts teach, when our autonomic nervous system is calm or even joyful, our thoughts can improve, and the meanings we make become more positive. Our bodies can rest, reset, and receive rejuvenation because nervous system regulation involves feeling safe in our bodies and environment.

For example, when we feel unsafe or like we're in danger, our bodies can enter a "survival state" instead of feeling calm or restful. When this happens, we can become habitually on edge, trying to protect ourselves from perceived harm, even if we're entirely unaware of what's bodily occurring. I speak from experience that to live in a chronic state of emotional angst—daily feeling anxious, depressed, sad, confused, stuck, deteriorating, or worse, like we're dying—is a terrifying and exhausting way to live.

Chronic emotional unrest is stressful, but thankfully, life holds something better for us. You matter! You are good, and YOU ARE CAPABLE. What can you do to help your body feel calmer and more at ease? Please list things you like that could ease your spirit, mind, and heart. Some examples include listening to music, making art, being creative, going outside, being with animals or pets, exercising, spending time with others, and so on. In other words, what do you enjoy that could help you feel more relaxed, fulfilled, or energized? Your well-being is essential. Please take care of yourself!

Day 11

Question: We've been working hard on this chapter. Yesterday, we focused on calming your body to aid your emotions, thoughts, and well-being, and you listed things you enjoy doing. Today, I ask: Is there something written down on yesterday's list that you could do? I know that may seem inconvenient, but please do it now if you can, and come back to write about your experience from that list. Why? Because I want you to FEEL in your body what healing and restoration are like, I want you to experience what joy, peace, play, or refreshment feels like in your physical body. Or, at the least, please reflect on something you've done from that list before and can recall. How did that event or exercise help to still your heart and mind, or enliven your spirit? Did that exercise relieve your stress or provide hope in your pain? Tell me about that experience, and if it was helpful, I ask you to please consider incorporating such practices into your life. Again, why? Because, believe it or not, when our bodies are restful, calm, peaceful, or content, we can experience life far differently. Friend, I want you to experience healing, a restful mind, a relaxed body, and an enlivened spirit. I'm rooting for you always! Please tell me about your experience or reflection on the next page.

Storytime

I've been examining my life for the past 20 years, trying to "make sense" of it. I've been on a mental and emotional journey that many would never venture into, but something in my spirit called me to it. I had to do it! Meticulously examining my life has not been easy, and at times, the pain is unbearable, but I am SO glad to be aware of the stories holding me back. For example, because of the trauma I told you about, I struggled for years with the false belief that I was ugly and unlovable. That false story hurt. Surprisingly, my healing came mainly through my body relaxing and the fear dissipating. I still struggle with other things, but my former adolescent trauma from losing the person I loved most was finally resolved, and now I can rest. Thank God!

Day 12

Question: Fear and insecurities can arise as we seek greater restoration and healing. Not to sound like a broken record, but this is likely linked to former or ongoing trauma since our fears and insecurities have to do with safety. How? Well, as I've already kind of explained, when we don't feel safe, we get scared. As experts teach, this is because our nervous system is activated when we're afraid, like when a white-tailed deer flips its tail and runs to keep itself secure. Similarly, we experience insecurities when we worry or feel "unsafe" that something in our lives could go wrong, especially when we don't want it to or if we yearn for something important.

Sadly, our fears can hold us back. However, as we heal, we need not let fear and insecurity rule us: you are stronger than your fear and more capable than your mind tells you. Dear one, what fears do you struggle with, and what insecurities do you have? By contrast, what would you like to feel in your physical body instead?

Day 13

Question: Now that we've discussed negative stories we tend to tell ourselves and the meanings we make based on the state of our body (i.e., whether or not we're in a fight, flight, or freeze pattern due to fear or insecurity), what areas of your life would you like to be healed? What needs to be restored? If I may ask, what has bothered, troubled, or hurt you for a long time that you would like to be healed from? Please note that you can be as heartfelt and specific as you'd like. While I feel timid asking because I know how sensitive these topics can be, it's important that I lean in and request; granted, it takes time, and I know it's difficult to believe, but eventually, the emotional pain points in our lives—the parts that ache, bleed, and hurt—can be restored. I myself never believed I would heal. I thought I was too broken and too far gone, but the peace and calm I feel now are incredible. Though it may be difficult to imagine yourself, I believe in you and your healing! Please write your thoughts and answers in the space provided, and bless you. May all of your wounds be healed.

Day 14

Question: In this chapter, we've thoroughly addressed false stories and the idea of reframing them into a more positive, holistic outlook. Yesterday, we discussed healing and what we would like to be emotionally healed in our lives. As we heal, we also mentioned that fear can arise. Yet, to heal, we want to feel inwardly calm and safe in our bodies. After all, the more peace, joy, play, and goodness we invite into our lives by doing things we like and enjoy, the more we can grow and be restored. **You Are Capable**, my friend! Thankfully, your emotional and mental well-being is possible—even if it takes time or feels uncertain. What will help you to believe that you can achieve your hopes, goals, and dreams? What will help you believe you're capable and that healing and restoration can be possible? I ask because I know it took me a long time to believe and trust in such things myself.

Tools

Before closing this chapter, I want to provide more tools for greater peace in your spirit and body, for more confidence in the process of restoration. Here are some resources that have brought healing:

1. Creativity and play can bring us joy and contentment. Not to speak overly about myself, but being creative has been central to my healing journey. I'm not sure how I would have survived without it, as art provided an outlet when I couldn't verbalize my troubles. Whatever you like to do—journaling, crafting, scrapbooking, singing, acting, dancing, cooking, gardening—whatever it is, please keep doing it! I'm convinced that art and recreation heal.

2. I would be remiss if I didn't tell you about Ignatian Spirituality since this is a "spiritual" self-help book. What is Ignatian Spirituality? It's a 500-year-old Catholic teaching on discernment that allows one to make better decisions in life with peace. Friends, I cannot speak highly enough of this teaching, which has, in no small way, transformed life by bringing more peace into my heart and mind as I consider weighty decisions and everyday struggles. I didn't know this theology existed, but if I had, it would have completely changed my life by helping me to discern with greater clarity and peace—and in my case—preventing specific traumas from occurring. I cannot speak highly enough of it. Thus, at the end of this book, I'll direct you to specific Ignatian resources for decision-making and living in daily peace.

Chapter Three

Self-Care

Y ou are lovable.

The goal of this chapter is self-acceptance combined with self-care, especially if you struggle to value your health and well-being. I know that self-acceptance can be incredibly difficult, as our minds and circumstances can tell us many things, suggesting we're unworthy and unlovable.

We mentioned that as we heal, fear and insecurities arise. Doubts creep in, making us wonder if caring for our well-being and health is possible or reasonable. Below is a list of objections people face while on a self-care journey. We'll name some particular challenges.

Main Objections for Self-Care and Holistic Wellness:

Skepticism about Effectiveness—people wonder if a book or exercise can truly help their life.

Time Commitment—we're worried the time necessary to study and implement can be too much and costly.

Fear of Overwhelming—we're concerned a technique or book may be too taxing to navigate.

Previous Failures—previously trying self-help or professional materials that didn't work creates a reluctance to try again.

Prefer Outside Help—there's often an emphasis on receiving professional guidance or the belief that healing mainly comes through structured support rather than self-guided material.

Low Self-Perception—many struggle with feeling inadequate, believing they won't effectively use the tools for their care, or view self-care as being selfish.

These are genuine concerns as we seek to care for ourselves and our lives. Over the next seven days in Chapter Three, we'll gently discuss life goals, needs, and boundaries, and we'll talk more about forming secure attachments (i.e., creating healthy, sustainable relationships). We'll also reflect on the concepts of self-care and thriving, while encouraging your self-acceptance (as opposed to developing levels of self-hatred) by focusing on "You are lovable."

Here we go!

Day 15

Question: Before beginning, I want to say I'm proud of you for working hard on your wellness. It's challenging to put in the work for greater stability and peace of mind. Thank you for taking care of yourself! You are valuable. This chapter focuses on self-care. Think of it as your opportunity to blossom or maintain your well-being to live the life God has for you or the life you desire. Something we haven't reflected on is what you hope for in life. Do you have goals or things you hope to accomplish? If so, what are they? Please list them and be specific. We're doing this exercise because pursuing passions, interests, talents, and life callings requires thoughtful reflection and, of course, self-care.

Closing thought: To be human means to have desires, hopes, goals, and dreams. Sometimes, our goals take years to realize. I told you I've wanted to write books and pamphlets since my 20s. Though I didn't know it would happen, I'm glad that yearning never left. What's inside you is vital. Please pursue your hopes, even if it takes 20 years.

Day 16

Question: As you pursue your goals, hopes, and dreams, protecting your well-being and having boundaries is necessary. Some of us are incredibly giving, to the point where we neglect our preferences and needs; sadly, we may struggle to VOICE a need or boundary. When this habitually occurs, it can erode our health over time. We can become a shell of who we were. My friend, I know it's hard, but it's okay to say no. Please note: you aren't responsible for everything. You don't have to say yes to all offers. Know who you are, what you stand for, and what you enjoy—and try not to fear disappointing others when honoring your needs. I humbly ask, in what ways do you struggle to care for yourself? What, if anything, do you need to say no to (again, I know it's hard, but you can do it!)? What matters to you that you're not currently doing? Do you struggle to care for yourself; do you sometimes think self-care is "selfish"? At the end of this book, I'll provide a resource about boundaries so that you can become more attuned to your needs, values, and even your yearnings.

Closing thought: Societal pressures can be overwhelming. For example, in Western culture, women often feel the need to be everything to everyone. Men may struggle to connect or express their emotions verbally. Unrealistic expectations hinder our eventual growth and, consequently, our care. Though challenging to receive, as much as the community needs matter, so do yours, dear one. After all, when you're whole and well, everything functions better around you.

Day 17

Question: So far, we've discussed life goals, considered our needs, and touched on boundaries. I would now like to return to the topic of secure attachments (i.e., forming healthy relationships). Why? Because the way we form relationships is critical for our ongoing health. As taught by attachment theory, disorganized relationships that are highly uncertain and chronically feel unsafe, avoidant interactions when we cannot address conflict or be too close from fear, or anxiously engaging with others (i.e., being habitually afraid to lose the other person), all of these relational patterns can be stressful and sometimes harmful. Life-giving interactions, by contrast—relationships that still, restore, or enliven us—are possible when our bodies are calm and our hearts feel confident in who we are, namely in the presence of the other person and vice versa. When this beautifully occurs, this is called forming a "secure attachment" because we feel safe with the other person and they with us. Again, I'll provide a resource about attachment theory at the end of this book so you can learn more about your specific relational patterns and how to heal your relationships. For now, what are your current best relationships, and why are they great? What are your worst interactions, and why are they presently not functioning?

Closing thought: It can be hurtful when relationships fail, but we flourish when they flourish. Not surprisingly, our upbringing establishes HOW we connect with others. Therefore, learning about attachment theory will help us better understand our personality and tendencies. Additionally, learning about the nervous system and how to regulate the body can help heal our "attachment wounds" (i.e., our relational wounds), allowing us to navigate our relationships better and hopefully transform our lives.

Day 18

Question: I said at the beginning of this book that I want you to thrive. So, if we can, let's now talk about thriving in the context of self-care. Thriving involves many components. Initially, I naively believed that thriving meant having external events in your life put in order so that you could experience joy. In other words, I thought that if all the externals in your life were functioning optimally, you could and would feel better inside. However, I now know through trial and suffering that life can be nearly destroyed, and all that matters is that you internally experience REST. Yes, your life can fall to pieces, but it won't ultimately harm you if you have peace as a baseline. Granted, it's good that your life externally flourishes, but if it doesn't for a time, you want to thrive regardless inwardly if at all possible. Our lives change when learning such wisdom. The hell you live in can become the portal to your success; ironically, the enemy of our souls is defeated as his insults increase our blossoming.

As mentioned, to thrive internally (not externally) means to have rest and peace inside and, when fully established, even joy. However, what would it look like for you to thrive externally? If you could imagine a bountiful, beautiful life, what would that be and look like for you? Please write down your thoughts.

Closing thought: Joy awaits those who've experienced intense suffering and hardship. Through suffering, I've come to believe a spiritual battle exists. May the enemy of our soul recoil. May you grow endlessly in this life and the next. I'm rooting for you (you're lovable!).

Storytime

I've mentioned I've been on an emotional journey for the past 20 years. Actually, longer. It's been 26 years! My self-reflection and healing journey began in my teens, and it's taken so long that much of the time has felt brutally SLOW. Not only have I been emotionally journeying, but it's primarily been a spiritual battle—one that I never expected to face. In fact, there's a lot of my story I'm not sharing in this book. Namely, I've experienced several traumas, not just one. Throughout, I learned the hard way that self-care and self-acceptance are essential through having both a mental and physical collapse in my late 20s and early 30s. While I don't know one hundred percent how life will unfold or what my future will precisely look like, I can honestly say at present my spirit, mind, and body are finally at PEACE. With peace, I can face my future with courage, living my present moments in calmness and stability.

Day 19

Question: 5 years ago, I embarked on a journey to thrive by identifying factors contributing to external flourishing. I called it the "7 Points of Thriving." Although I did not thrive, the factors I identified were accurate. Thus, I ask: What are the essential elements people need to achieve stability and growth in life? What are the obvious daily routines required to function and flourish? What do you personally need to thrive? After writing those things down, please identify an area you're lacking and consider if you could grow in self-care by pursuing it. Example: Perhaps you've wanted to take better care of your physical health for a long time, but haven't. Now, you decide to start.

Day 20

Question: Caring for ourselves isn't easy, especially if we think it's wrong to practice it. Why might we view self-care in that way? Many sincere voices teach us to give and serve, which is excellent. However, an unbalanced interpretation of that message can come at an expense. While giving is certainly valuable, habitually giving from an empty cup can be dangerous. When fully and exhaustively spent, we can no longer provide. For some, this manifests as us having a health collapse or a "mental breakdown" since, in certain instances, caring individuals over-extend themselves. While it's important to love and serve, wise application is needed, or the scale of our fruitfulness can unintentionally topple.

Dear one, have there been times in your life when you've given too much and it has unnecessarily cost you? Please reflect. What did that experience do, and how do you now balance your commitments? I genuinely ask, can you both honor your very real needs while also honoring and considering what you can genuinely provide? How can your cup stay FULL to keep living, enjoying, serving, and being? Please list practical examples from your life. Also, please note that tomorrow will be the end of our 21 days, but more content follows in the rest of the book :)

Closing thought: It's okay to take care of yourself, my friend. When you do, you can better live and be more yourself. When you're fed and nourished, that goodness overflows. Getting sleep, exercising, and the like aren't silly. They keep us going! Your attention to your health and growth doesn't just benefit you; it benefits others.

Day 21

Question: Congratulations! We've made it to Day 21. We've been on a journey together, thoroughly examining our lives. You've done a lot of self-reflection in these past days to promote your healing, and we've focused on your care for the sake of your present and future. Your present moment matters! You matter, and **YOU ARE LOVABLE**. While it may not seem apparent, this chapter is overall about self-acceptance. I know how hard it can be to value and accept oneself, as I once struggled deeply with self-rejection and self-hatred from the former adolescent trauma I told you about. Self-rejection is excruciating, but the more we can accept every aspect of our being and genuinely take care of ourselves, the more goodness we can invite into our lives. Yes, take care of yourself, dear one, so that more peace can enter and a thriving life begin. I'm rooting for you! You're valuable. Your internal peace and rest can and will lead to your external reward.

What were these past 21 days like for you? Did you have any revelations? Did anything become clearer? If so, please write that down. Finally, what do you hope to take from these 21 days of reflection to implement in your life? Please note that if you need more space to write, there's more room on the back of the next page. Bless you, and may all your dreams come true.

Tools

What final tools can I leave you with to promote your inward thriving, self-acceptance, and external blessing? Let's see!

1. I'd like to recap the tools already mentioned: getting out-doors and being connected to plants and animals. Learning about the nervous system so we can heal our wounds. Making art and being creative to keep us in the present moment. Learning about Ignatian Spirituality to help make decisions with peace. There!

2. Another personal note I haven't shared is that I grew up Protestant and studied systematic theology (in addition to dance performance). I recently converted to Catholicism. Why? Because, as life would have it, tools from Catholicism began to heal me as my life further fell apart in my unsuccess-ful, 5-year attempt to thrive—externally. These tools helped me to thrive inwardly. So, I'll share them; there are sever-al. They include novenas, learning stories about the saints, reading the Apocrypha, studying Marian apparitions, and being consecrated to Jesus through the Blessed Mother (i.e., Marian consecration), as well as learning about sacramen-tals, attending Mass, receiving the Sacraments, and more. I honestly never thought Catholicism could help me in any way, nor did I know that I had misconceptions about it. My journey won't look like yours, but nothing has brought greater peace into my life than having God's love calm my body and heart. May peace find you, too!

Closing

Thank you so much for journeying with me throughout these 21 days. It's true that I've asked myself all of the questions in this book countless times since I've been on a self-reflection, self-healing, and self-care journey! In other words, I unknowingly spent years preparing for this book because I've had you in mind and heart.

It's worth noting that I would have healed much faster if I'd known what I know now. For example, for many years, I didn't know about trauma and what it does to the body, mind, and heart. Because of this, I didn't know HOW to get out of my trauma, so I stayed stuck in a fight, flight, or freeze pattern for nearly two decades. Since there are several traumas I didn't relay in this journal, it's taken a long time for me to heal—and I imagine you may relate.

In a nutshell, I struggled to believe that I was good, capable, and lovable. I thought the opposite for so long, and that hurt badly. I'm SO happy to share this message my priest emphasizes because it gets to the heart of my battle (and the struggle of so many): loving me as God loves me or loving you as God loves you. If I came out of my journey healed and nearly whole, I know you can, too! I'm rooting for you.

With love,

Tessa

P.S. You are good. You are capable, and **You Are Lovable.**

Resources

Often in books, the resource section is formally written. I'm going to speak in the first person because I want you to take these tools to heart. Below is a list of resources I utilized on my healing journey. Some of these resources have been invaluable. Even if they're unhelpful or inapplicable, there are so many healing modalities. I know you'll find your way! For what it's worth, this is what has helped me:

1. Local parks for recreation, beauty, and play. Scour your area to find the most incredible, life-giving landscapes to enhance your joy and well-being.

2. Engaging in creative and artistic endeavors. Art speaks, and art heals. Find what you like and do that if you can.

3. While many resources teach about the nervous system, I've been most connected to the work, workshops, and classes offered by Sarah Baldwin. Who is Sarah? Sarah's an expert in nervous system regulation and has studied with the best in the world. A personal note: for years, I prayed, *"Lead me to the best,"* and I was led to Sarah and a few others. Sarah's worked with thousands of people and has a unique, practical way of breaking down how to get in the "driver's seat" of your

thoughts, emotions, and actions. She teaches boundaries, attachment theory, and much more. My trauma has largely been healed by working with Sarah through her courses, "Navigating Your Nervous System" and "You Make Sense," and by participating in her online workshops. Knowledge of the nervous system in relation to trauma healing has been taught for the past 30 years, and Sarah began offering her courses prior to 2020. She knows what she's talking about! You can freely listen to her podcast, "You Make Sense," on YouTube and visit her website, sarahbaldwincoaching.com, to learn more. You can also follow her on Instagram @sarah-bcoaching.

4. Another invaluable resource was learning Ignatian Spirituality from Fr. Timothy Gallagher, which has helped me make decisions and live more peacefully. Who's Father Gallagher? Fr. Gallagher's an expert in Ignatian Spirituality. He's written several books and hosts multiple video series on YouTube, teaching the "Rules for Discernment" by St. Ignatius of Loyola—a saint who lived during the Protestant Reformation. Do you struggle to make decisions in life, especially big ones, or to have daily peace? I didn't know this theology existed. If I had, it would have completely changed my life by preventing specific traumas from occurring. Sadly, I learned about it too late, but I use it now! You can find Fr. Gallagher's books on his website at discernment.institute. You can listen to his video series at discerninghearts.com. Specifically, there's a 16-part series on YouTube I highly recommend titled "The Discernment of Spirits, Setting the Captives Free" and an 8-part series called "Discerning the Will of God." These are

both fantastic resources for any Christian or anyone who struggles to make decisions, especially significant ones, or who struggles to find, maintain, or experience daily peace. I cannot speak highly enough of these videos, which are designed to calm our troubled spirits and set us free by bringing Christ's peace into our lives.

5. By the way, Ignatian Spirituality pairs remarkably well with studying the nervous system. The two go hand in hand! Beyond these things, people and resources you trust can help you heal. Bless you.

Bonus Material

What Is the Nervous System?

One thing I didn't do in this book was define the nervous system. I'll try to do that now. Again, I'm not an expert. That's why I direct you to the experts, but I'll try my amateur best since it's worth explaining.

What is the nervous system? In the womb, the brain and spinal cord develop. The nerve endings stretch to our fingertips. When you're fully grown, outside, standing on a breezy day, the wind brushes past your arm, touching your mammalian skin, and it sends signals through your body to your brain. Throughout life, when you breathe, you do so unconsciously; when your heart beats, you don't think about it beating. Nonetheless, it does so to keep you alive.

What I'm trying to communicate is we're designed with a brain, spinal cord, nerve endings, organs, bones, tissue, skin, and so forth. Our bodies pick up the information we receive from the outside world and begin to process and calculate it automatically. Often, we aren't even aware of this. In fact, in formal studies, the "nervous system" is broken down into several components, including the Central Nervous System and Peripheral Nervous System (which includes the autonomic nervous system).

As taught by experts regarding nervous system regulation, throughout your life, your body has the job of keeping you safe. That's part of what your body does. If we think of animals living in the wild, they're always looking out for danger or harm to stay alive and survive. Humans do the same thing. We just aren't nearly as aware!

What I'm saying is your body is constantly, automatically looking out for harm (or peace) in order to protect you. If you hear an alarming sound, your body responds. If you smell a pleasant fragrance, your body reacts and relaxes. Again, these things often occur without us even knowing or acknowledging, unless we're self-aware or grow in this capacity.

The beautiful thing about learning about nervous system regulation and the nervous system is that **you** can better understand and recognize when your own body is going into a fight, flight, or freeze pattern due to external circumstances and what to do about that automatic bodily response. Or, by contrast, to distinguish fear from, say, a physical, bodily reaction of peace.

Our body responds to trauma in this way: it goes into a fight, flight, or freeze pattern when it feels it's in danger or potentially in danger. For example, if you experience daily anxiety, your body is reacting to something, even if you can't understand it. In likeness with, say, ongoing depression, the body is responding, even if we can't initially comprehend what's going on or why. What I'm trying to communicate is that your body "speaks" BEFORE the mind. Your gut reaction occurs before understanding and comprehension. That's why when you feel peace, which is a somatic response, it's a signal of rest and ease.

Thus, learning about nervous system regulation from someone well-trained can help put one in the "driver's seat" of how they feel, think, and respond, as it teaches us to be aware of what's happening in our bodies related to external events and developing skills to manage or comprehend those innate responses, instead of dismissing them.

Undoubtedly, this information can help with relationships, our life goals, feeling rested, raising children, and calming our spirits and minds. Learning about nervous system regulation can be a game-changer since this knowledge allows us to become more in control of our emotions, actions, and well-being rather than being tossed about by things we cannot understand, perceive, or act upon. In other words, it can give us superior insight and thus agency; it can reveal the wound to hopefully bring about the cure.

I hope this brief explanation can be helpful. Again, this information, combined with Ignatian Spirituality, was life-changing for me. That's why one of my goals for this journal was to help you feel GOOD—and at rest—in your body, mind, and spirit, so that peace can come into your life. Why? Because when we feel peace, we feel safe. When we feel safe, we can rest; when you rest, you can feel joy. When your body is no longer frightened, on edge, angry, scared, sad, or depressed, you can heal. Holistic healing is possible for you!

After working through this journal, I deeply hope that your body, mind, and nervous system can gradually calm so that you can feel better, happier, whole, and more alive. Christ said, "My peace I leave with you," may it be yours.

Acknowledgements

I want to thank those who have stood by my side, helping me to heal and never giving up on me. Thank you for giving me the strength, guidance, and support.

Additional Disclaimer

The author wishes to express and encourage you to be in the driver's seat of what you take in, learn, and receive. In other words, not even the experts always know what's best. Therefore, the information provided in this book is meant to promote your well-being, but you're the one who gets to decide what's appropriate for you and your life.

This book reflects the author's personal experiences, research, and understanding. Readers are encouraged to seek their own support where and when needed.

About the Author

*Tessa dancing outdoors in 2019. This Bio will
make sense upon reading the journal. Enjoy!*

Tessa grew up in the United States and has always been spiritual. Her faith means a lot to her! She's had many desires throughout the years, but has struggled with emotional, physical, mental, and spiritual health due to complex trauma. Tessa dances outdoors and loves to do that, and she's passionate about people healing and knowing God's love. As you can tell, she wants people to experience peace and joy.

Specifically, Tessa studied dance as an undergraduate and received her M.A. in Systematic Theology in 2010. Since 2016, she's been creating art and sharing her life story through the work of *Inner Reformation*. Her mission is to "help people find safety and peace in their body, soul, and mind so they can hear and receive from the Lord to live a life of peace, joy, and love—to have their lives put in order to flourish, grow, and thrive" (Parable of the Sower and Song of Songs 2). Overall, her hope is for people to live a life of peace.

Tessa dancing in "Inner Reformation"

Since 2019, she's been working on her written autobiography after dancing out her life story in 2018. Her greatest desire is for people to know God's love, love Him back, and for Him to bring us good (Jeremiah 32:36-41). Tessa especially desires to help "make the soil healthy," as she calls it, so that people can GROW and thrive. The way to do this is through having a regulated nervous system so that the body and spirit can receive, for example, the peace and love of God. She deeply longs for healthy individuals and families, for people to come to faith and lives to be changed entirely, healed, and restored. How? By bringing Christ's peace through powerful stories of redemption.

These are some of her greatest desires, but why? Well, believe it or not, Tessa's had this desire for over twenty years, ever since losing the person she once loved most as a teen. When she lost that person, she intimately met Jesus at age 18, and her life changed dramatically; an "Inner Reformation" began to occur when she gave up that person so that God could give her all He had for her. Why did she give that person up?

In short, the person she once loved most discerned whether or not to become a Catholic priest beginning in 2001. Nearly 25 years later, in 2025—the year of Jubilee—Tessa herself was brought into the Catholic faith. It's been a wild, painful, heartbreaking, unexpected, beautiful journey of learning to know Christ's love and loving Him back with all of her heart.

The author in August, 2019

Above is pictured Tessa on her first outdoor dance experience, which helped to heal her relationship with herself. You can learn more about Tessa from her website, innerreformation.org. You can follow her on YouTube and Instagram @innerreformation, where she dances outside, shares her story, and offers viewers a sense of peace, play, and joy. God bless you!

Author's Note: *You've just read a more personal bio than usual, since parts of my adolescent story are woven throughout this journal. My hope is that, after journeying through the pages, you'll see how it all fits together—that the bio serves as a continuation of the journal itself.*

INNER REFORMATION
JOURNAL SERIES

A work of Inner Reformation

Created to bring peace, clarity, and healing
to the mind, body- and heart.

Dedicated to those journeying *through*
pain — *toward* peace.

This book is part of the Inner
Reformation movement.

A soul-centered invitation to wholeness.

INNER REFORMATION:

A Video Companion to this Journal

A *friend suggested that I consider creating a video companion so* *people can see me and feel more of my heart. I was privileged to listen to this friend's story over the course of several months. Thankfully, my friend felt seen, more understood, and validated regarding her life's story and the trauma she endured. It made me so sad to hear of her suffering and the injustices she experienced, often created by systems intending to care for her but failing. When we experience trauma, we usually struggle to make decisions and get trapped in patterns that further perpetuate our pain. It can then become challenging to break free from those mechanisms, but not impossible.*

Both my friend and I believe in your healing, and we long for con-tinued restoration. May the following videos be a blessing to you as we seek to hold your hand; may they provide comfort and food for thought upon your completion of these 21 days. ***The journey continues :)***

Videos One, Two, and Three can be found at:

innerreformation.org/videocompanion

www.ingramcontent.com/pod-product-compliance
Lightning Source LLC
Chambersburg PA
CBHW051330120626
46547CB00016B/2475